·FRANCE·

·FRANCE·

Michael Ruetz

Introduction by Hubert Comte

Bulfinch Press · Little, Brown and Company

BOSTON · TORONTO · LONDON

First English-language edition

Introduction and captions translated from the French by Martin Roberts.

ISBN 0-8212-1780-1
Library of Congress Catalog Card Number 90-55222
Library of Congress Cataloging-in-Publication information is available.

Frontispiece: *Roof detail, château de Chambord*
Title page: *The Georges-V bridge spans the Loire at Orléans*

Bulfinch Press is an imprint and trademark of Little, Brown and Company (Inc.)

Designed by Carl Zahn

Published simultaneously in Canada by Little, Brown & Company (Canada) Limited
PRINTED IN JAPAN

This book is dedicated to the great novelist Louis-Ferdinand Céline

—*"C'est pas le tout d'être rentré de l'Autre Monde"*

Introduction

Our country: a name we learn to say, later to write; an image on a map someone shows us, so beautiful it seems almost unreal. Some countries are landlocked, France only partly so. Its borders are natural: land abruptly comes to sea, plains to mountains. Some of its boundaries are impassable, others have had to be constructed. Over time, the country has expanded and contracted, like a beating heart, but it has managed to find a balance between the two.

From time to time, indeed, France has been tempted beyond its borders, but historically it has tended, as in nature itself, to trace watersheds, lines of separation. The reason is simple: we follow a certain path until we realize, from the shape of church towers, the layout of fields, the way people greet us, the color of shutters, that we are not at home anymore, and so we go back.

How do we discover our country? How do we acquire our conviction that *this*, strange as it may be, is still part of us, whereas *that* is not?

One discovers France through the French themselves: through cousins, at weddings, from work or study. The process begins with the first camping trip or bicycling holiday to a lake in the Jura, a fortified town, perhaps a stay with relatives who live in Brittany, or the Landes, or the South. Changing landscapes gliding past a train window; different houses, different soil, fields, trees. Roman tiles beyond a certain point, or the white gables of Breton houses. Gray slate roofs in the Loire Valley. Dovecotes in Normandy. The houses of Alsace with their crossed beams.

As new passengers board the train, we discover new accents, new physical types, new forms of dress. Conversations say a lot about the work people do and the things that matter to them. In the Périgord, one overhears earnest discussions about mushrooms, as if people were discussing the procession of the Magi; in Burgundy, people inquire about the alcoholic content of the year's new wine.

Visiting friends put pressure on us: "I've already been to see you, but you never come to see me. There's plenty of room for you. Why don't we fix a date?" When we do finally go, captivated by the Lot Valley, or the Saintonge region, or Alsace, we regret not having done so sooner.

Like lily pads on a pond, the regions we know spread out and touch one another. Literature plays its part. From Daudet, we learn about Provence, from Pagnol, Marseille; Giono conjures up the countryside around Manosque; Mauriac vividly evokes the pine trees of the Landes, oozing with sap; Genevoix's poachers could easily persuade us to stay in Sologne; Péguy surveys the plain of Chartres; Blondin offers us his quai Voltaire. . . . And there are many more.

Wherever we go, our fondness for our own region travels with us, yet we are also attracted by others because we have chosen them; because, in a way, they counterpoint us.

Soon, new images arrive to focus, magnify, and clarify our view of France: Courbet, keeping a watchful distance from the wildness of the Jura; Corot, contemplating the stirring of trees in the Ile-de-France. Van Gogh stalks the countryside around Arles, paint box on shoulder. Matisse, Bonnard, and Renoir explore the South. Monet studies the play of sunlight on stone in Rouen before moving to Edenic Giverny. Fautrier paints wild mountain scenes at nightfall in ever-darkening shades of gray. Utrillo charms us with his views of Montmartre. . . .

One day, quite by chance, we discover the world of food and drink. Our discovery may deepen into an appreciation that lasts a lifetime, as, time and again, we rediscover that a fine meal is one of the best things life has to offer. A father takes his child down to the cellar to choose the wine: it is a chance to learn something new, among the shadows and the cobwebs and the dank smell of the soft ground underfoot, so irresistibly evocative of secret passages and hidden treasures. And there they are: the bottles, with their colorful labels, their light and dark collars, their characteristic shapes. The solid champagne bottle, built to withstand high pressure, topped by its mushroom-shaped cork and splendid collar of gold foil. As the cellar man rightly said, "as wines go, it's pretty straightforward: you don't even need a corkscrew, just somewhere to chill it." Alsace bottles too are easily recognized by their river green glass and slender, heron-like profile. The difference between a Bordeaux and a Burgundy can easily escape the unpracticed eye, but one soon learns what to look for: the bottle of the first has well-defined shoulders, whereas that of the second is more tapered, like a raindrop. Meat, fish, game, dessert—which wine goes with which? In passing, we might be shown a special bottle covered in a thick layer of dust: "I bought this one the day you were born; we'll open it on your twentieth birthday." How far-off that day still seems! Key in hand, we go back up the steps, reflecting on the remarkable patience of grown-ups—and of wine.

In addition to the wine cellar and the kitchen, the dining room and the restaurant, appreciating French food and wine is partly a matter of word association, since every place has its own speciality. The associations come up so often in conversation that children soon know which places and specialities go together before even savoring the delicacies themselves. They become like a litany, as automatic as the replies in the game of *Pigeon?—Vole;*[1] anyone seeking to pass himself off as French would give himself away at once if he hesitated over them: Bresse?—blue cheese. Saint-Nectaire?—cheese. Dijon?—mustard. *Choucroute?*—Alsace. Brie?—Meaux. Saint Menehould?—pig's trotters. Cider?—Normandy. *Calissons?*[2]—Aix-en-Provence. Foie gras?—The Périgord. Cavaillon?—melon. *Socca?*[3]—Nice. Bouillabaisse?—Marseille. *Pauchouse?*[4]—Verdun-sur-le-Doubs. Lyon—*saucisson. Kougelhopf?*[5]—Alsace. Strasbourg?—sausages. Tripe?—. . . à la mode de Caen. Nougat?—Montélimar. *Tome?*[6]—Savoie. Mushrooms?—Paris. . . .

[1]A children's word game in which one player gives the name of an animal and the other has to say what it does: "Pigeon?" "—fly." "Fish?" "—swim," etc.—Trans.

[2]Diamond-shaped sweetmeats made from ground almonds.—Trans.

[3]A flour made from chick-peas in the Nice region, from which is made a kind of flat cake sold on street corners.—Trans.

[4]A Burgundy matelote (fish stew) made from a selection of pike, gudgeon, eel, perch, or carp.—Trans.

[5]A light, brioche-style cake made in the shape of a narrow-brimmed hat with a hole in the middle, decorated with sultanas and almonds.—Trans.

[6]A type of cheese.—Trans.

In short, any serious collector of France's gastronomic riches will soon know the country itself, its highways and byways, its villages and towns, as intimately as any seasoned geographer.

Lost in his epicurean daydreams, our geographical gourmet might well be brought abruptly back to reality one summer's day by the sight of an imposing red barrier set up at an intersection watched over by two gendarmes. If he asks why the main street is closed, and whether it will be closed for long (since if so, he would prefer to retrace his steps), he will be told that "it" is passing through in twenty minutes, and that everything will be back to normal in half an hour. Of course! How could he have forgotten? The Tour de France! Already, indeed, the main street is packed on both sides with fans of the exuberant, unpredictable cycle race, with its sorrow and its glory. The annual spectacle of the media circus, of the sleek champions flashing by on their spindly machines, and of the sports commentaries all add to this summer craze of young and old alike, whether interested in sport or not.

But there is also a more relaxed, more sedentary contest, which evokes a different side of France: *boules*. Rival teams compete to see which can produce the more devastating shots, which can outmaneuver the other in the closely studied playing area. Players and onlookers keep up a running commentary on the successes and failures, but hold their breath at the crucial moments, when stakes are high. Deep into the night in the little towns of southern France, one can hear the musical voices and the clink of the metal *boules*. So what's the purpose of it all? The pleasure of community, the chance to have a few drinks together, perhaps even to settle amicably an old dispute between neighbors.

School vacations with family or friends are an opportunity for small children to discover the blueness of water, the whiteness of snow, and for their elders to experience anew the excitement of speed, the pleasures of physcial activity. From such personal experience, they will begin to appreciate the wonderful variety that lies within their country's borders.

But all good things come to an end, and the yellowing leaves on the chestnut trees are a quiet but firm reminder that classes will soon be restarting. As everywhere else in the world, it is in school that children learn most about their country. In geography class, first of all, we learn to draw the familiar outline, then to trace the main rivers with our finger, to identify the cities and the characteristics of different regions. We accept without question everything the teacher and the book say; one day we will see for ourselves the port or vineyard we have heard or read about. Occasionally, indeed—and such moments of recognition always give us pleasure—we might find ourselves in a place we know already, so that everything seems real on two levels at once: this port in Brittany, this peak in the Alps, this volcano in the Massif Central, are familiar to us already.

Knowing a country's geography also means knowing its climate: the heat and sometimes the high winds of the South; Alsace, snow covered and silent in winter, often baking in summer; the persistent drizzle, but also the spectacular sunbursts, of Brittany. Wherever one goes in France, the words spring, summer, fall, and winter take on different meanings, bring different images to mind. Is it any wonder that its inhabitants should be so diverse in their ways of speaking, tastes, ideas, interests, and life-styles?

History, too, can tell us a great deal about both the upheavals and the great shared experiences of the past. At first sight, history might seem less in evidence in the provinces than in Paris, where it is on view in every square, on the walls of every building. Taking even a short walk in the French capital is a bit like watching a speeded-up movie. Halfway down the Boulevard Saint-Michel, the old Roman baths, the Thermes, stands guard like a fortress. Farther on is the Sainte-Chapelle, recalling the story of Saint Louis. Notre-Dame, the medieval masterpiece that figured in one of Victor Hugo's novels and witnessed the joy of the Liberation. The Louvre, home of kings. Part of the wall from the celebrated Bastille, and the square of the same name. The Place de l'Étoile, a legacy of Napoleon. The Opéra, built for Napoleon III, at the end of its wide avenue. A moving commemorative plaque on the wall of the former laboratory where Pasteur carried out his research. The recently opened arch at La Défense. . . .

But history has also left its mark on France's villages and towns, especially in the provincial capitals. A Romanesque church; a war memorial; perhaps a local castle, with its still-active legend of a secret passage, evoking the alternating lavishness and harshness of feudal times. The seat of the provincial Parliament; a historic battle site; the statue of a famous person, maybe even the house in which he or she used to live. . . .

The vitality of the French language abroad, making life easier for the French traveler, also reveals historical residues and spheres of influence. French is spoken in Belgium and Switzerland, but also in Quebec, numerous African countries, Martinique, and Noumea, and it may even still be heard in Pondicherry. . . .

Even abroad, the French will continue to discover their country. They might never have imagined that anyone could associate them with perfume, high fashion, and elegance. But they will return with this chic, glamorous image of France, the France of seduction, reflected in the envious gaze of others.

All this, then—all our chance discoveries and our intentional ones, all that we have learned and experienced, all our dreams and accomplishments, all the people and the obstacles we have encountered, all our pains and pleasures, our delights and disappointments—all this is woven together into the rich tapestry that is our knowledge of our country. Every cast of the net is rewarded, every lamp picks out a new tree in the darkness, every balloon sails over a new hill, every raft sweeps down a new river. Put all the experiences, the knowledge, the quests, and the discoveries together, and you have the image of a country, a memory that will endure.

And then one day, these shifting fragments of memory, the simple places we remember so fondly, the landscapes to which we long to return, are rediscovered in a book. . . .

Hubert Comte

Author's Note

Italy is the origin of Europe, our umbilical cord to the world of antiquity, to Greece and to Egypt. Great Britain is the museum and America the future of Europe. What is Germany? The heart? Hardly, despite our being in the heart of the Continent. That turns out to be nothing more than a fluke of geography. Are we the head? Preferably not.

Let us then remain somewhere on the edge. Let us turn our eyes to that vast region to the west of us. For us, France is The West. It has the wide-open spaces of the West. Behind each hill is another cultural microcosm, another European delight. Apart from matters geographical, therefore, France is the center and heart of this formation in ways that transcend politics and economics. It is this "formation," Europe, that I belong to, much more than to an ever-stronger Germany.

My generation oriented itself—curiously we don't say "occidented"—toward France long before America was in fashion. Whatever made life more worth living, that could be learned or experienced in France. In France one does things with subtlety and ease that in Germany are done only with gravity, solemnity and silliness, and gobs of state funds. The *History of O* was written in France—by a woman; our great "orgies" were pulled off far from our eastern borders by male beings; they are not part of a novel but brutal, inerasable history, the "History of G."

The reader of this book will see none of that here. Instead there are wide spaces in which I love to be. We call them "landscapes." Paris is too narrow—I have chosen to photograph it with a bird's-eye view, to make it appear as a broad cityscape. Invisible, but for the "feeling" eye nevertheless "visible," are the many films of Truffaut and others that I always carry in my inner eye—*Goupil Mains Rouges, Quai des Brumes, Marius,* and *Les Enfants du Paradis.* Moreover, what has trickled into this book is another work that I consider part of my own personal fabric, that I have read over and over: *Voyage au bout de la nuit (Journey to the End of the Night)* by Louis-Ferdinand Céline. Céline, with his German leanings, was never at peace with his nation; neither have been I. Céline was always aware of the moon—as am I; I devoted a whole book to it. His melancholy look toward the horizon is also my look, and there have been many moments in which I have felt like his hero Bardamu. Céline has put his stamp on my image of France as has nobody else. The afterimage of that stamp is to be found on the pages of this book.

Michael Ruetz

Munich, March 1990

Michael Ruetz, *Self-portrait, September 9, 1989*

22

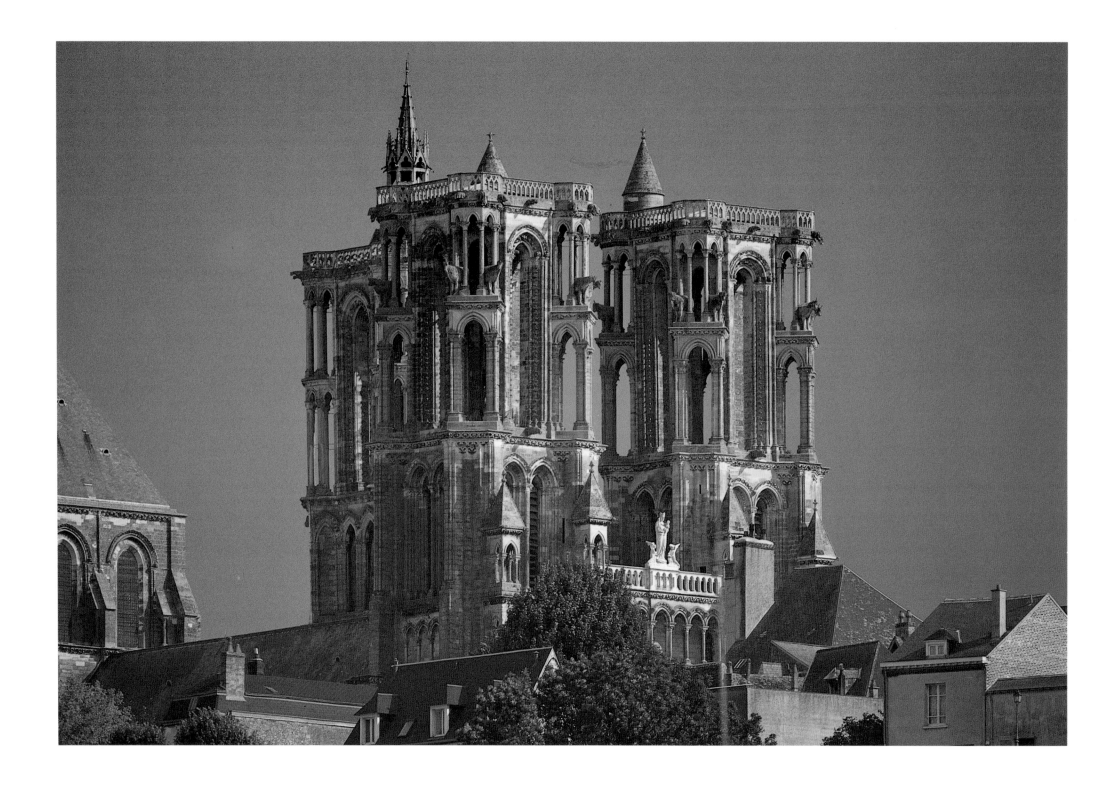

137

List of Plates